Morning Moon

Morning Moon

Poems by

Laura Schaeffer

© 2025 Laura Schaeffer. All rights reserved.
This material may not be reproduced in any form, published,
reprinted, recorded, performed, broadcast,
rewritten, or redistributed without
the explicit permission of Laura Schaeffer.
All such actions are strictly prohibited by law.

Cover design by Shay Culligan
Cover image by Firdous Parray on Unsplash
Author photo by Jeff Ellett

ISBN: 978-1-63980-798-7
Library of Congress Control Number: 2025945731

Kelsay Books
502 South 1040 East, A-119
American Fork, Utah 84003
Kelsaybooks.com

"Absence is a house so vast
that inside you will pass through
its walls and hang pictures on the air."
—Pablo Neruda

Acknowledgments

Thank you to the editors of the following journals in which these poems first appeared.

Collective Visions: "Carpenter Lake"
DASH: "Moth"
Hole in the Head Review: "Redrawing the Company I Keep," "On Memorial Day," "Days of Eden," "If This, Then"
Medicine and Meaning: "Summer Ash"
Pif: "Morning Moon"
Pitkin Review: "Then Arjuna Asked"
Poetry Corners: "Across Fields"
Tidepools Magazine: "Expansion"

The author is deeply grateful for the friends, teachers and mentors that have offered their invaluable feedback and encouragement to me throughout the years. I especially want to thank Lauren Davis, Sarah Townsend and Tristan Beach for their help in providing editorial feedback for this book, along with large doses of support and encouragement. Thank you to my children, Jess, Jeff, Randy and Brian, who shared in many of the experiences in these poems and have continued to inspire me with their resiliency, joy and love of nature. To my family and our many sea days together, both near and far. And to Kelsay Books for their support in helping me to give voice to our common losses through this experience of my own.

Contents

And Grief said	13
Teach Me How to Walk on Water	15
Boswellia	16
His Sabbath Poems	17
Sarai's Prayer	18
Days of Eden	19
Samaritan	20
Of Magdalene	21
Approaching Night	22
Borderline	23
Fishing	24
Arnica Cordifolia	25
A First Walk	26
In a Vase	27
Redrawing the Company, I Keep	28
Mantra	30
Malaise	31
Foghorn	33
A Found Negative	34
Yellow Plum	35
Gratitude	36
Dandelions	37
Then Arjuna Asked	38
Summer Ash	39
Of Lavender and Light	40
Meeting Light	41
Indescribable Light	42
There's a Time When They Stop	43
Weavers	44
Recovery	45

There You Are	46
A Narrow Space	47
A Last Forgetting	48
Two Roads	49
Camouflage	50
Every Night Now	51
The Artist Upon Finding a Dead Robin	52
Vacant Lot on Newberry Hill	53
Floorboards	54
Moth	55
A Poppy Is Just a Flower	56
Little Bug	57
The Master	58
Wednesday	59
Mustard Seed	60
Wind Chime	61
Bus Stop	62
On Memorial Day	63
Carpenter Lake	64
Across Fields	65
Expansion	66
Coyote	67
Late Summer	68
If This, Then	69
Conch Shell	71
Morning Moon	72

And Grief said

from a breath stone

—underearth

I will never leave you

submerged

fully condensed

with human love

Hold me—

there is room.

Teach Me How to Walk on Water

I want to be a phenomenon
lighter than I've ever been.
Fearless, without a yesterday
or want to dream. Unaware of caution.

Make me a northern light
that bends with waves.
A part of the sun touching earth remotely,
then retreats back within itself.

That's the way to be, isn't it?
Sometimes or once in a life.
Without any rope tied to a ski boat,
just slalom style over the liquid night.

Boswellia

She said you should've seen the sunset making stained glass in the
   trees.

With a full glass of wine left on the kitchen counter, a list of to-dos
turned faced down. Marlboros abandoned, she said:

There's a floating raft nearly deflated on the couch,
also, dried eucalyptus in a vase, aloe vera at a windowsill,

jade and cactus. Rilke is opened on top of the Bible,
bookmarked at the portal poems and God whispers in pages

I will make you my wife forever. Jezreel—
if you just look around as God told you,

you can see the uprooted turmeric and ashwagandha leaves
steeped in a teacup. After all the determined distilling,

after all the goodbyes that honestly, never stole any fragrance,
you are still able. Carry the remedies to that far-off garden.

Boswellia for the ache of reaching.
Frankincense resin to the prepared room.

His Sabbath Poems

after Wendell Berry

If I could only better envision them—
your long walks out on a Sabbath
through marshland and stubble;
farm fields spread out with whatever
was said and said again
like seeds falling between rows
of each sloshy step
and the redwing's flash towards home.

If I could only meet where the blueprint drapes
a whole sky to its footstool—

I'd come rushing,
quick as this morning's fawn
leaping laps in and out of the kingdom
on this day of commanding play

to bring my prayers down.

Sarai's Prayer

I want to take an ax to joy
lift the blade overhead
and come shattering down:
splitting a core
dividing a cell
since we agree
conception begins with halving.

Are we such small gods?
I would like to murder joy
for every birth
for every starlit night
for each space I cannot fill.

Days of Eden

There you were by the willow we named
one crushed daisy under foot
and hair that had never been cut falling over your breasts.

All we could hear were birds.
All the light was a silence we could break
with just a move or motion of smile.

We had few words in a garden that stretched further
than we could ever see. The surprise of each other's voice
echoed off the bark of created things.

Your form adorned the day more than color.
A body mine and not mine.
I followed you, hidden as a snake.

Peaches on a branch burn with ripeness
and the wonder of sunsets clothed in leaves
is a brilliant joy, a sweet fuzziness.

I have watched you at sleep before
beneath the willow's tentative hand and the lengthy
shadows darkening us.

Breaking the silence, I move always closer
wanting to wake you—
say a name I do not know.

Samaritan

There he was—a stranger
standing in the dirt with sandals,
his dusty feet strapped
and a tattered hem.

From Jacob's well he spoke to me
a Samaritan, a woman. He asked for water.

I looked back to the windows
of our village,
afraid that someone was watching,
Muriel or Esther or Hada.

There was no one.

Of Magdalene

Even your body disappears—
the last chance gone
to kiss your feet.

I washed you with myrrh,
with that thorny shrub on rock
piercing my hand.

I smoothed aloe into each crevasse
taking my time to worship
skin that was still yours.

Here I am, Jesus
carpenter, man of sorrows
who entombed me.

Even before daylight—gone
and no one but an angel
celebrating your return.

The rock rolled aside for this—
a cave and shadow of your face
on cloth?

I feel nothing.
Seven days to grieve you
and this eighth to prepare for joy.

Approaching Night

I take your hand and it is late.
The sky is cooled ember.

I won't know where you have gone

if we've walked too far into woods
and you let go

becoming only thin air.

I would be looking back,
thinking this was the place—

a moment ago
when you were still here.

Borderline

Gabriel, it is too much horror.
Look how the line quivers
there at the horizon.

Look there at birds scattered dead
all along The White Sands
Missile Range.

A pall bearer carries them in hand.
One-by-one back to the bird cemetery
with wings in a palm.

What do I know of a sky falling?
You must have slipped through that line
to tell us of terror and beauty.

Fishing

My sister's machine breathes for her.
I watch her chest breathe
like a tackle box.

And rivers move through her
carrying someone else's blood,
who must act quick

to reel and cast.
Who must act quicker!
Who must be quickest!

to hook and net.

Arnica Cordifolia

While we are waiting for one war to end,
another begins and wildflowers pass over.

You were both canary and medallion shade,
born of shallow sand for a fragile life.

All this time I thought you were something else.
The thing to be cut down, a mere weed.

Never once did I suspect your rush to injury
or how it was possible you'd open vessels

on my back hand, where the blood bruised
in old attempts to clot my indifference.

A First Walk

I am not pretending in beauty.
The hospital had a face half-covered with ivy.

As I pushed you in a wheelchair through the garden,
you directed me. You said over there—there!

echinacea in bloom
and we stole it for the nightstand.

In a Vase

Uvalde, Texas

Thinking of her
he picked daisies
along the highway
where she would accept them
into her hands
and with her hands
fill a vase of water
to be placed near dreams
to touch one another
in dreams
rise and tap
the thin hemispheres
of glass.

Redrawing the Company, I Keep

The white circle was drawn in black ink.
With black ink I redraw a white space.

At first, I see the space growing.
It is hard to keep up,

to round back the dark,
though it becomes thinner and not like forever

where things get lost.
There are three people between Mars and Pluto

standing upright without any ground.
It is between time without hands that point,

their long and short unevenness
blocked by light. I only sense a gravel road.

In space we think there is void
but it is not true.

We think silence is silent
when it hums incessantly in a foreign air.

I chose a mother to pull up weeds.
I chose a sister to dig up clams

and if that wasn't enough to befriend a domain,
another sister to rein in her horse.

They were wearing white gowns,
which I hated because it made them invisible,

except for their faces, laughing faces
that seemed to look over a badminton net,

waiting and ready for the return
red rubber volley.

They dropped their hand tools
and the horse galloped wildly towards me,

a black and white body
that swung its mane with a nod,

turned backside, bowed a neck
and crunched the full light

of thistle and shell.

Mantra

Outside the window of her hospital room,
on the ground floor
where steam was seeping from a vent
in all the streams of May;
with scent of our grandmother
coming nearer
from the nearby rose garden,
I said, *I'll see you later.*

I'll see you later,
over and over
in hypnotic mantras.

I'll see you later,
as many times as one is sure.

Malaise

The earth—

she seems out of tilt.

I shared quiche and grapefruit with you.

Without taste

we thanked God for it.

You have a condition.

It is the same condition

I believe

I have.

I called my brother-in-law

after you left.

He has it too.

I called my son who has it.

My daughter born on this very day

who also has it. A co-worker

sick at home

that has it.

Her dog.

Her cat.

The earthworm unable to move.

The beetle

in bed.

The fir

with white moss.

Even the slope

the slant

are gravely steeped.

Birds are dropping

like flies and

there goes a bobble head

down our lacquered

Bourbon Street.

Foghorn

somewhere

only a boat measuring land
avoiding shoreline
while sending out signals

somewhere

only a girl in mist
draped over branches
of a pale Spanish moss

A Found Negative

From a window I watched her clutching.
She had a rolled-up beach towel in arm,
a walk of hurry through dunes,
as familiar as a motion picture.

A storm was still passing through,
leaving engulfed tide pools
with floating plastic bottles
and lighters that had sunk in neon.

Rain spattered the glass in pizzicato,
then bowed in a downstroke of silent rivers.
She had found a high place to shake out her towel,
look to the sky before sunbathing in its dim light.

Within minutes, as a new thought arrives,
she rose. A child being resurfaced within me
and with mirror to see through to a past time.
She began to run, a girl, over pools to the surf

and without hesitation waded into water
wearing only shorts and tank top for a swim.
Where are the sisters? The mother?
The girl was head and arm in surf,

half a body in water and light,
half a dream that shifts sand
upon waking and pulls out time.
Lost, found, loss ongoing

as the moon's spare change:
quarter, half, full, newly pressed
to begin over with. There were faces.
There once was touch.

Yellow Plum

Crinkled pond
of iridescent wing—
dragon breath.

I go to the evening's curled fern.

Above
broken sky
silent hemlock.

Gratitude

for Holly Hughes

There are birds growing quiet and moths visiting.
Waves beyond the dirt road
rush the cliffs
arriving from an ocean of dark night.

Because two books will arrive tomorrow
and a poet lost her computer, then found it,
I asked if her heart was pounding.

Because it's graduation for my nephew
who will go on adventures
and I am away from the news in this hollow.

Because the Libra moon seeks a balance.
Maybe, that most of all. I'm not sure,
but someone helped me today—

the sky was all blue.
Who knows what it means.
I want to stop sometimes.
I want to say go.

Dandelions

An unusual blaze burns on the dry bank.
A center of yellow fire
alive as a community of Pentecostals.

Each slender, leafless stem is upraised
to its inverted umbrella aura
drunk in a sun worship.

They seem possessed by a uniform light
that blurs and sways, heady
beside a blue heaving sea.

Then Arjuna Asked

Atman, if you can save me,
then tell me how to lose shadows
attached to my feet
or the mimicry of each warrior's act
echoing behind and before me now.

My dharma divides between fear and love.
My sword is double-edged.

This little fog will pass.
It is nothing but an eyelid
closed over a green vase
where
the bloom and drinking
stem lived

so fragrant
in an old room.

Summer Ash

You could fly for an instant
whole body in separate hands
cupped and held hands.
You could fly when they let you

but I made a mound beside me
to keep your shoulder to my shoulder
to lean into wind to feel an updraft
of your paper bone.

Of Lavender and Light

I have been feeling a light beneath me,
as if my body were not sunk in gravity,
as if I have become rootless.

I look to the tops of trees
because my windows are high on the wall
and the view of birds reach in motion
as a sea where waves roll by.

Here at the pond is a stillness—
creased paper fallen from a desk,
a splash of frog between lilies,
and strands adrift from curves of talons.

All that is midway being etched into water—
all the undefined substance of things made Vermeer:
temporal home,
woven twig and remnant.

Perhaps, I am uncontained,
outlier of my own breath
or light reflecting off branch.

I borrow the wings of bees
swarming their lavender honey.

Meeting Light

I dig ditches with my bare hands
and dirt is jammed beneath my fingernails.
I toss out the large rocks
and pause to watch worms hide.

This tunneling is compulsive.
It doesn't matter what I wear
because of the darkness
because of solitude.

Underneath foundations of homes
roots slow me down
forcing my body into thin turns
like detours threading.

And above me the ground thuds
with a walking on my head
as a trespass stomping heels
of community in aeration.

Light streams through holes
that pierce all the way through me.
It comes as a sudden pain to my eyes.
All my crawling stops in its glare.

Indescribable Light

The moon rose up through the trees
climbing up along silhouettes and strings
simple as an ant's investigation
and slow and deliberate
sensing the watcher of small things
from a porch through a lens.

It was soon forgotten. Silent,
the moon went about its destination
without any worry of darkness or insult
coursing the heavens
the same as it always had.

There's a Time When They Stop

Sudden silence with no easing into it.
A grave time, when gravity
catches the wing.

They must circle a dial then,
for every morning they sing again
and with no holding back—

roused to berry, worm, and thunder.

Weavers

With the smallest of wings and claw,
their beaks open to an overflow
and structure too, for the pattern.

They cut through air, darn new pathways,
pull loose threads as if we can't see the loom
outstretched over sky

that each day they are willing to reveal:
our arms and legs entangled; bodies
draped by some fluttered good will.

Recovery

I draw evening and morning—
Hard snow. Bird tracks.

I draw sticks on a fence.
One dimension of things.

Looking over my shoulder,
I draw your breath in glove.

Third base wait.
Homerun slider.

Can I miss your smile just a little?
Your two-armed hug?

Summer boy,
before the fall?

Can I miss your Subaru days
as much as you do?

There You Are

on the same back porch
with the same birdsongs
while the world has pivoted.

You watch the spring light
after hail after sun
asking for the same promise
which arcs in its prism now.

And I see you, myself,
removed from myself
and I sing the slate blue, sing
each dying as my own treble chord.

We have been two, you stranger, you as I.
We have been multitudes. We, one.
Only trees know.
Only down to their roots.

A Narrow Space

Can I ask you
to move closer
here
beside the window
of your lake?
I want to feel
the summer breeze slip by
with light combing
each wave.

A Last Forgetting

How very small a thing goodbye is
when it comes on an October day.
Maple leaves burn behind the house
then fracture in sparks of turning light.

How small an ending comes
with its gradual weakness
clutched at a branch. The sway
of deciding against a deepening night.

I think I can remember
and still, there is the last forgetting
chosen on a wind's lip,
twirling like a girl's brown skirt—

a time
so small now
I can cover it with a rake
or let it lie mute
before the first descent of snow.

Two Roads

Frost was right then,
about divergent roads—
meeting there eventually
and being forced to decide.
I think of Dorothy and her dog,
rows of corn stalks gone dry
in the face of cheery sunflowers.
How she wanted to know the way home
and how those ruby slippers,
with so much magic wrapped around feet,
simply paced between road signs
                    for days and days in dreams.

I wring my hands that way
or this way, as she did—only
deciding not to be dazzled by Technicolor
gloss and the brainless bird-cawing crow
pointing a road there. How would he know
the far far away someplace
and something?

Lions and tigers and bears! Oh my!
Lions and tigers and bears! Oh my!

Where is there no place like home?
Here or there? I clang my way
with an echoing tin of what was:
a smooth bedspread, a dog in arm.
Auntie Em keeps calling my name,

but I hardly hear myself now
and yet, see a thing far off,
as if a drowsy beetle were starting out,
full of a lion's courage
on a road less travelled.

Camouflage

I have failed to remember death as a return,

as water slipping through a culvert's vein

with a gurgle of swift absence.

Here, on the arc of a wooden bridge,

I see my face camouflaged

beneath the floating weed.

Every Night Now

The pond is the same darkness.

Lilac branches have thinned to arthritic fingers.

The clematis has fallen on her side breaking a hip

and still,

she clutches at the trellis with brittleness.

The Artist Upon Finding a Dead Robin

For the first time
      I can hold the absence of flight
           here, in my hand.

Eyes black stone.
Flies burrowed in chest—
lifeless
      unclutched
           dangle.

I hold a brush
to shoo a charcoaled buzz. I set
in towels
      on a compost stench
           a tawny breast.

Empty
      Waned
           Skying . . .

Your last yank on worm.
Your last song, tilt in current.

I found you sideways on the front porch.
Dead as abandonment.

Now, daffodils rise from the grave
      spilt in their trumpet memoriam
           Come back!
                Come home!

Daffodils, that hold yellow
           their little while
                as you held blue.

Vacant Lot on Newberry Hill

Everything is returning and passing again.
You, riding a motorcycle through a field
where the old barn slopes and the split paint
lifts off from the inner walls.

Remember the mattress we peered at, cupped
to hands to see through to window and shadow?
The sheetless fade of dahlias on a sunken bed
and the shoebox turned down

creased with tissue,
were like lines marked in our palm,
with what led us here
and what turned us away.

Floorboards

Ghosts were so thin last night
they squeezed through the grains of wood.
I'm sure of it.

The wind pushed into windows,
but nothing spoke.
Around me a nothingness looked on

that was more familiar than a face
or a patterned knock at the door,
heralding voice in an off-note.

It was not hello, I said.
There was nothing to say
that had not already been said

from a past to now.
This word in longing that crowds me,
that steps without sound across floorboards.

Moth

When you rest that way
it reminds me of an Egyptian pyramid.
Your wings fold into a triangle on a rail
full of porchlight. A barometer of weather.

I consider my gurus
of which you don't know.
It is easier for you to be still without words.

You are the shade of bleached driftwood,
the color of blond wings
with their jagged argyle bands.

I promise I won't exchange this moment
for anything more than your hair strand of legs,
your breath that settles deep into a universe of unbound time.

Yes, I want a little night bathing light.
Yes, you want a small word that returns everything lost.

A Poppy Is Just a Flower

A poppy is just a flower
with a drowsy head.

Deer in the yard avoid its seeds.
Round and round sniffing, and to prove

the poppy's unmistakable scent
we buy mixed bouquets,

pulling the poppies out
one at a time

because they are first to droop.

Little Bug

Tell me, the world
what distance means.

In an open book
you are a capital size

back cover and down spine
skating a gloss.

Tell me the lettered history
of our human loss.

If they were the boats
from which you float.

If you smelled the rose
pressed hard to nose

or heard the last word wrote
from some tattered note.

The Master

All of the oil paint had dried,
though it seemed continuous
as a sky living. Sun in a corner
and slate stone clouds.

I watched the light make a bevy of doves,
then empty them onto a branch. In the foreground,
crows, sparrows, a finch half darted out from briar
as if startled by worlds.

The cyclone fence was in ruins, sloping and bent.
Maple leaves and grass tangled in wire.
It was winter. A woman in a skirt nearly climbed
stairs out from the field, leading the eye.

She seemed to hate the scene for being drawn—
sketched and coated, captured at last. A single strand
of horsetail was left absently on her face. No reach possible.
Nothing to be touched without the master.

Wednesday

The rain is just rain
traveling for miles,
as if to finally announce,
Look, where I've been!

I've heard this rain before.
I've heard some things move so fast
an eye doesn't notice.

Some words are this way too.
They seep right into roots
and the trees—they wave back.

Part of rain is part of my own thought
lifted to fall, an inaudible race
back towards the permeable.

Only it sits on my nose whole,
damp with its globe,
its window and mirror.

Mustard Seed

I am mistaken for the poppy.
I am that tiny.
I can fall off your thumb
if you sneeze
and though I can be shades of cheerfulness,
I am at times
the belly of a copper pot—
the cooked color rust
burnt to a black tar.

When you believe mountains move,
are you mistaken too,
by needles falling from a sky blanket,
foil found on a bedroom sheet
or trails polished aluminum
along their sharpened veins of dreams?

Wind Chime

I'm not sure if the bells were ringing,
but I heard them for two years,

always the same, not made up.
I heard them after each death.

There were times my name was called.
Someone calling for me who knew

I was listening
who I was

but couldn't precisely find that.
So, I hung a wind chime.

Bus Stop

We stand behind the wet bench,
away from the gutter.

Some of us hold umbrellas,
others wear parkas with hoods.

One old woman wears a dress coat,
her chin hanging nestled

in the fur collar, her hair
covered with a plastic hat.

She's waiting too.

All of us look up the road.
All of us with a place to be

waiting for the ride to take us there.

On Memorial Day

From here they fly out—fly in—
temporal moorings of tide and sea mist.
This, on a day of remembrance

when you sat at the kitchen table eating toast.
You were so real to the ordinary
with your talk of faraway places, and

almost gone. Was it for honor, Soldier?
Was it escape from our boredom?
Barnacles can breathe under the weight of water.

Held tight, with home somewhere attached to rock.
But my silence is caught in sail, hovering at a ledge—
with an absence holed up in chest like a bullet.

Carpenter Lake

The raised boardwalk is already weathered.
Two years of rain have stained cedar planks
to the lightness of driftwood.

Pewter wings of a heron let go from a snag.
Drop, glide low
over the lake's surface.

Everything mute in palette;
beige stalks of last summer's cattails,
dried moss, chalked and clinging.
Dying that holds for another season.

You point towards the overgrown trail to your home,
towards the hidden canoe waiting a release from vines

and with a sudden urgency turn,
press hard against my lips.

Across Fields

The wind howls through the valley
lifting snow and sculpting ice banks
walled along the river.

White firs lean in
bowing side-to-side
loosening their coats.

Though night spreads out across the fields,
I follow tracks left behind.

Expansion

Last night a woman laid down on the railroad tracks.
Her body became flint steel. The train
screeched until it finally stopped.

It was a beautiful day.
A festival had been set.

For the rest of the evening
the ferry returned onlookers
to their boxed cars and homes of every color.

Gaps between islands widened.
Low groaning engines reached the galaxy.

Coyote

The green belt is where I imagine you most.
Both of us together on a concrete lot
looking for hours at the UFOs.

We ate June salmon all month,
which caused a fire in the oven,
leaving us both unclear ever since.

You thought you were taking care of me
each time we moved on to another house,
but I knew you were.

I scraped bones off a pan and then threw out the pan.
We're a long ways away now.
Coyote on another mound.

You just packed yourself up one day
and the bells stopped ringing.
Wherever you are, they might ring.

How'd you know I turned inside out?
Even from your kindergarten face,
hard as the rain I stood in

streaks on you.

Late Summer

Here at the pond the sky is closer. Trees show their watery faces

    with wide open. My own reflection merged.

Layered light and shadow build and dissolve. From one moment to the next

    color wobbles, blending into unnamed hues—rings of beige

layered in pine needle, rim of seed, torn thread. Salamanders and water rats

    rush out from the iris and sniff. Their faces gleam in elongated pewter, in a pond

    sinking as if by earth's thirst.

Cells bloom.

Trunks narrow in reduced frame. Line and post. Green

that is, not its becoming. Rippled circulars of untouched and touching.

I watch a portrait.

Watch face into sheets.

My own arriving and departure.

If This, Then

there are strawberries to be eaten.

In a refrigerator a pound of butter,
cheddar cheese, raspberry yogurt

and I am misspelling again
on my list of things to acquire:

abbreviations and grapes.
I think of dairy cows grazing.

From there I think of pastures and around them
sloping posts tied with barbed wire.

I think of sunlight and exaggerations.
See for yourself how loose they hang.

A cow's eyes don't make a statement,
but a question not to be bothered with

as the jaw swings left to right.
I've begun to stutter, mispronounce

as if I am speaking out from a cud
in swell and sway.

If I had a pasture instead of a refrigerator,
then there would be no need.

All day chewing answers indifferently
in a soft limp photosynthesis.

Flies in the eye. Hard hoof.
Enough space between dandelions

without need to open a pickle jar
using two hands.

But you wrote stroke on paper
before falling down stairs

and I've since picked up green beans

that slid to the floor.

Counting my numbers by one
by two, by three, by four . . .

Conch Shell

Flamingo Jim once sold me a snail house off Highway 101.
Inside you can discover your fate and believe it.

Waves continue ashore with their invisible city of dunes
as sound to ear.

If I once was there, I met faces.
If I can hear waves, I can hear voices.

My sister had a lion there
whom she imagined was friendly.

My brother bought a tumbling machine
to polish his eyes like agates.

We were all building turrets and moats
with an open window to the first words spoke

sight to voice.

I wanted to befriend hieroglyphic strangers,
trace my finger over sand script,

claim in the golden spirals
gods and angels, mythic dragons,

cedar bark, weeping willows,
poppy fields, glacial slides,

all home half on land
half a timeless sea.

Morning Moon

Slipping fingers into pastures where the horses rested
the mountain range grew sharp and haloed.

Sun was expected and a duty, to announce
our need. But you, lesser light, disappearing,

showed a way out
or what I think of now

as a way in
so that turning a corner

down past the clearing
on the road

I was equal
to my silence.

About the Author

Laura Schaeffer is a graduate of Goddard College's MFA Creative Writing Program and has taught workshops to alumni, college students, and new writers at community centers, including a poetry project for underserved teens, in which she obtained grants to produce a CD of their work. Laura has attended the Centrum Writers Conference on a full scholarship and continues her interests in international poetry and nature. She lives on the Olympic Peninsula in Washington.

www.ingramcontent.com/pod-product-compliance
Lightning Source LLC
Chambersburg PA
CBHW030912170426
43193CB00009BA/824